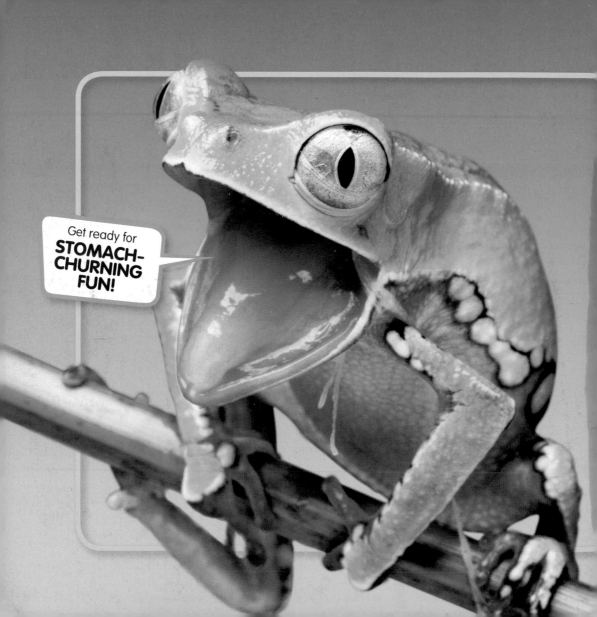

NATIONAL
GEOGRAPHIC
KiDS

Just Joking GROSS

Rosie Gowsell Pattison

NATIONAL GEOGRAPHIC
WASHINGTON, D.C.

300 hilarious and disgusting jokes, tongue twisters, riddles, and more!

4

In Bracken Cave, near San Antonio, Texas, U.S.A., a colony of 20 million bats has created a massive pile of guano, or poop, that's estimated to be at least 59 feet (18 m) deep!

Q What's green, weighs a hundred tons, and lives at the bottom of the ocean?

A Moby Sick.

Say this fast three times:

The Duke puked cukes.

Q What do you call a **teacher** who **doesn't pass gas** in public?

A A private toot-or.

SPIDERTOWN

Q Why did the spider go to college?

A To become a web designer.

KNOCK, KNOCK.

Who's there?
Snot.
Snot who?
I snot this was my friend's house, but it's definitely snot.

Sometimes when hedgehogs encounter a new smell, they will "anoint" themselves with it. This involves licking the new scent and then covering themselves with frothy saliva.

7

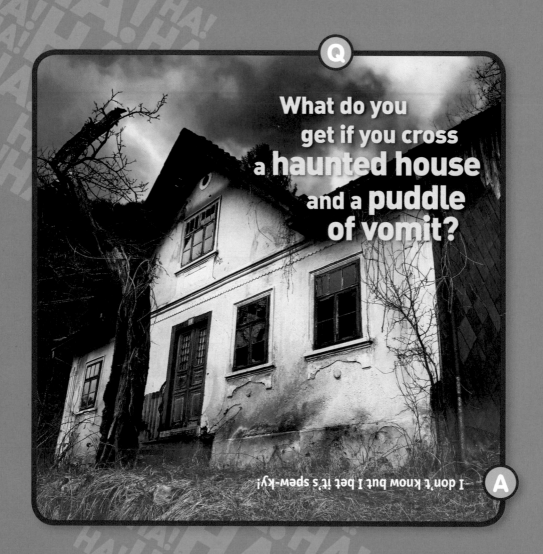

Q

What do you get if you cross a **haunted house** and a **puddle** of **vomit?**

A

I don't know but I bet it's spew-ky!

Q What do you call it when a COW breaks wind?

A Dairy-air.

Q What sport does an elephant play with an ant?

A Squash.

9

PATIENT: I don't feel good. What's wrong with me?

DOCTOR: Well, you have a piece of pizza in your ear and a banana in your nose ... I would say you're not eating properly.

TONGUE TWISTER!

Say this fast three times:

Mimi inexplicably is mimicking Mike's hiccupping.

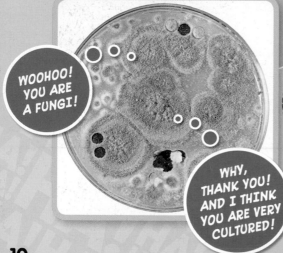

WOOHOO! YOU ARE A FUNGI!

WHY, THANK YOU! AND I THINK YOU ARE VERY CULTURED!

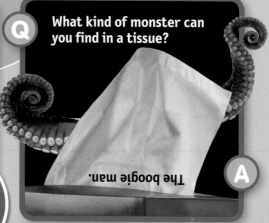

Q What kind of monster can you find in a tissue?

A The boogie man.

A male proboscis monkey uses its fleshy, bulbous nose to attract a mate.

Grossest of the Gross

Die Käsemilbe

12

OFFENSIVE OFFENDER:
Wacky Cheeses
FOUL FACTS:

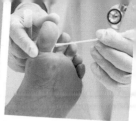

Ever wonder how cheese is made? Normally, the bacteria in milk from animals such as cows and goats—and even horses and camels—is the number one ingredient. This bacteria causes the milk to ferment and harden, and then it is seasoned and aged. If you think that's weird, these cheeses are even weirder: In Dublin, Ireland, researchers created cheese from bacteria collected from belly buttons, feet, mouths, and armpits. These unique-smelling cheeses were put on display at an art gallery, and guests were invited to take a whiff. Or if bugs are your thing, give *Milbenkäse* a try. *Milbenkäse* is a German cheese that has been fermented with thousands of dust mites. The mites secrete an enzyme that ripens the cheese, then the mites are eaten along with it. That's *nacho* average cheese!

Cheesemakers in the United Kingdom produced a Stilton cheese made with real gold.

Epoisses is a cheese so smelly, it's not allowed on public transportation in France!

Pule is the world's most expensive cheese. It's made from donkey milk and can cost more than $1,000 per pound (0.5 kg).

13

WHAT?

14

15

SNAIL 1: How was school today?
SNAIL 2: Awful. Two snails got into a fight on the playground.
SNAIL 1: Oh no! What did the teacher do?
SNAIL 2: She let them slug it out.

Funny names for passing gas:

- The Benchwarmer
- Butt Yodeling
- Fire a Stink Torpedo
- Heinie Hiccup
- Thunder From
  Down Under
- Bum Burp

Q

What happened when the dog started digging in the garden?

A

He soiled himself.

17

Q What do you get if you cross onions and beans?

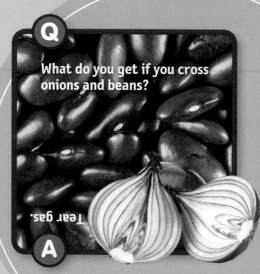

A Tear gas.

TONGUE TWISTER!

Say this fast three times:

A big black bug bit a big black bear.

Q What do you find in a clean nose?

A Fingerprints.

Q What do you get if you cross a skunk and six eggs?

A A very smelly omelet.

18

When a tokay gecko wants to escape a predator, it can detach its tail and make a getaway.

KNOCK, KNOCK.

Who's there?
Maggot.
Maggot who?
Maggot tells me I'm knocking on the wrong door ...

19

KNOCK,
KNOCK.

Who's there?
Dewey.
Dewey who?
Dewey have time
for a shower? I'm
really sweaty.

Sloths have thick fur coats that
are usually covered in algae. The
coat is also home to a type of
moth that feeds on the algae
and burrows into the fur.

20

What does a giant praying mantis eat after having its teeth cleaned? **Q**

A The dentist.

Gross TALK

WOOHOO! 5 MINUTES AND 30 SECONDS, THAT'S MY BEST SLIME YET!

A star-nosed mole has 22 fleshy tentacles at the end of its snout that act as a sensory organ. The mole is completely blind and uses its impressive schnoz to find prey.

23

TONGUE TWISTER!

Say this fast three times:

Juliet ate a jar of jellyfish jam.

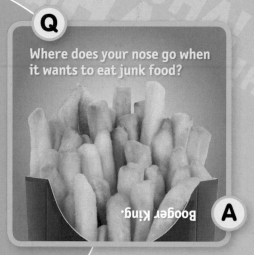

Q Where does your nose go when it wants to eat junk food?

A Booger King.

Q Why are toilets fun to be around?

A Because they are the life of the potty.

Q What do you call tired insects?

A Sleepy creepies.

24

Grossest
of the Gross

OFFENSIVE OFFENDER:
Fulmar Bird

FOUL FACTS:

Stand back! Get too close to these cute baby fulmar birds and you could end up with a face full of puke glue. That's right, these innocent-looking chicks are capable of projectile vomiting a bright orange oily secretion all over any would-be predators. The chicks have surprisingly accurate aim and can shoot repeatedly. Not only does the vomit stink like rotten meat, but it is very hard to wash off. It glues the feathers of predator birds together, making it difficult for them to fly away, or worse, impossible to swim. Not even mom and dad are safe—the chicks will open fire on their parents until they learn to recognize them at about three weeks old.

The name fulmar means "foul gull."

The adult fulmar's feathers are immune to the chick's vomit.

The horrible smell of the vomit is an alert to the fulmar parents that a threatening incident has taken place. Mom and dad can detect the odor before landing in the nest and may keep a watchful eye before returning.

Q

What do you call a **dog** chewing **old,** **stinky** sneakers?

A

An odor-eater.

I LOVE FAST FOOD!

Gross TALK

A chameleon's tongue is almost twice the length of its body and can shoot out of its mouth at around 13 miles an hour (21 km/h) to catch unsuspecting prey.

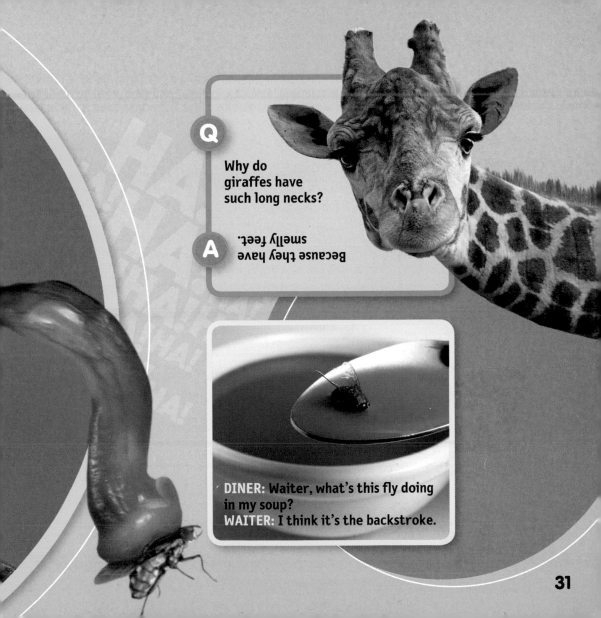

Q Why do giraffes have such long necks?

A Because they have smelly feet.

DINER: Waiter, what's this fly doing in my soup?
WAITER: I think it's the backstroke.

31

GROSS TALK

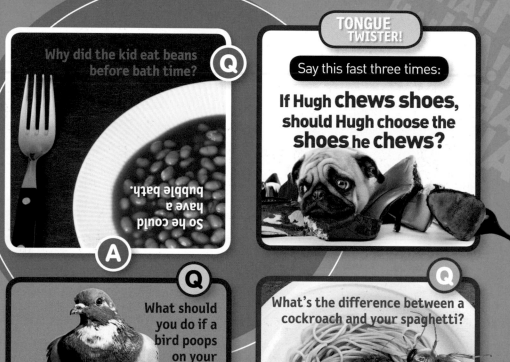

Q Why did the kid eat beans before bath time?

A So he could have a bubble bath.

Say this fast three times:

If Hugh chews shoes, should Hugh choose the shoes he chews?

Q What should you do if a bird poops on your head?

A Be grateful horses can't fly.

Q What's the difference between a cockroach and your spaghetti?

A A cockroach won't slip off your fork when you eat it.

34

Ancient Egyptians believed that dog drool had healing properties.

KNOCK, KNOCK.

Who's there?
Spittle.
Spittle who?
Spittle late, but I made it!

35

Q What do you get if you cross a pig and a toad?

A A warthog.

Q What do you get if you cross a **rooster** and a **toilet?**

Cock-a-doodle-poo.

A

36

Natives of Madagascar
believe the aye-aye is the
bringer of misfortune.

NAME **Lefty**

FAVORITE ACTIVITY
Surprising people

FAVORITE HANGOUT
The bathroom sink

PET PEEVE **Rolled-up newspapers**

Q Why did the zombie throw up after dinner?

A It's hard to keep a good man down.

BLECH! O-POSITIVE ... I PREFER B-NEGATIVE.

Gross TALK

40

KNOCK, KNOCK.

Who's there?
Slime.
Slime who?
Long slime, no see!

The hoopoe bird secretes a fluid that smells like rotten meat.

41

PIRATE: Hey, doc, how much will you charge me to clean out all my earwax?

DOCTOR: About a buccaneer.

Q

What kind of soda does a toad drink?

Croaka-Cola.

A

Funny names for barfing:

- **Multicolor Yawn**
- **Spill the Groceries**
- **Tossing Cookies**
- **Downloading Dinner**
- **Gale-Force Burp**

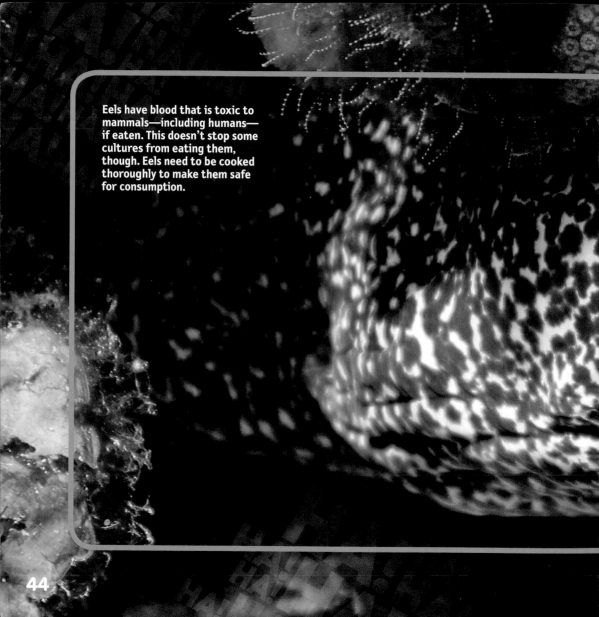

Eels have blood that is toxic to mammals—including humans—if eaten. This doesn't stop some cultures from eating them, though. Eels need to be cooked thoroughly to make them safe for consumption.

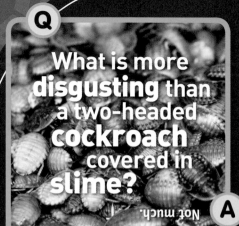

Q

What is more **disgusting** than a two-headed **cockroach** covered in **slime?**

A Not much.

Q How do you know when a turkey passes gas?

A Stuffing shoots across the table.

Q What do you call an envelope full of stinky toenail clippings?

A A nail file.

KNOCK,

KNOCK.

Who's there?
Interrupting burp.
Interrupting Bur—
Burrrrrrrrrrrrp.

Sheep tallow, which comes from sheep fat, is used to make soap.

47

IS THERE SOMETHING IN MY NOSE?

Gross TALK

Q

What do you get if you cross a candle and a cob of corn?

A

Earwax.

48

Bug 1: Did you hear my brother flew into the windshield of a car?

Bug 2: Really? When did that happen?

Bug 1: Splatter-day.

49

OFFENSIVE OFFENDER:
Dung Beetles
FOUL FACTS:

What do they do with all that doo-doo? Adult dung beetles use dung, or manure, from other animals as food. Female dung beetles use patties as a place to lay their eggs. When the beetles find a dung pile they like, they enjoy it in one of three ways: Rollers break off chunks of poo from the pile, shape it into balls, and roll it away to bury it—these balls can be up to 50 times their own weight! Tunnelers dig a tunnel under the poop pile and move some of the tasty poop inside. Dwellers burrow right into the dung and nest within or beneath it. All this poop moving helps recycle nutrients back into the soil, as well as clean up piles of patties lying around.

Dung beetles are picky: They prefer omnivore poo because it's the stinkiest. *Mmm.*

Dung beetles like their feces fresh. A scientist observed 4,000 of them attack a pile of elephant poop within 15 minutes of it hitting the ground!

One African species of dung beetle uses the Milky Way as a navigation system. After rolling a dung ball, they stand on top of it and use the light from the stars to help guide them—and their poop—home.

Q

What do you get if you cross a skunk and a really good book?

A

A A best smeller.

52

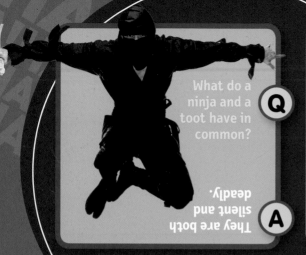

Q What do a ninja and a toot have in common?

A They are both silent and deadly.

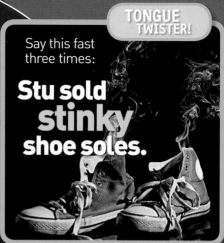

Say this fast three times:

Stu sold stinky shoe soles.

Q Why didn't the comedian tell jokes about breaking wind?

A Because they really stink.

Q How do you talk to someone with bad breath?

A From really far away.

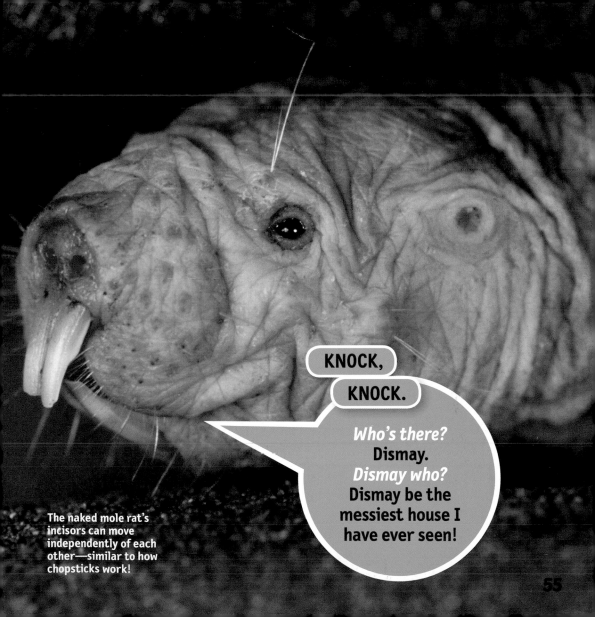

The naked mole rat's incisors can move independently of each other—similar to how chopsticks work!

KNOCK, KNOCK.

Who's there?
Dismay.
Dismay who?
Dismay be the messiest house I have ever seen!

55

The red-lipped batfish can't swim! This pouty-faced fish uses its fins as "legs" to walk around on the ocean floor.

CAN I BORROW YOUR LIP BALM?

GROSS TALK

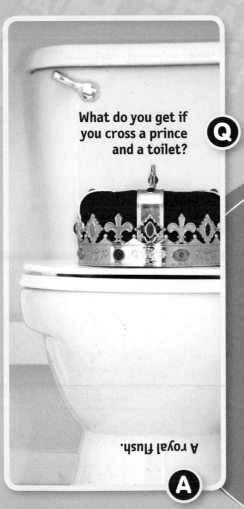

What do you get if you cross a prince and a toilet?

Q

A royal flush.

A

Where do you buy **lunch** at a **morgue?**

Q

In the cadaver-teria.

A

57

Chimpanzees chew up leaves to make sponges that they then use to soak up water to drink.

59

Q

Which day of the week do you pass the most gas?

A Tootsday.

GHOUL BOYFRIEND: I have a surprise planned for our first date.
GHOUL GIRLFRIEND: What are we doing?
GHOUL BOYFRIEND: We are going out for a three-corpse meal!

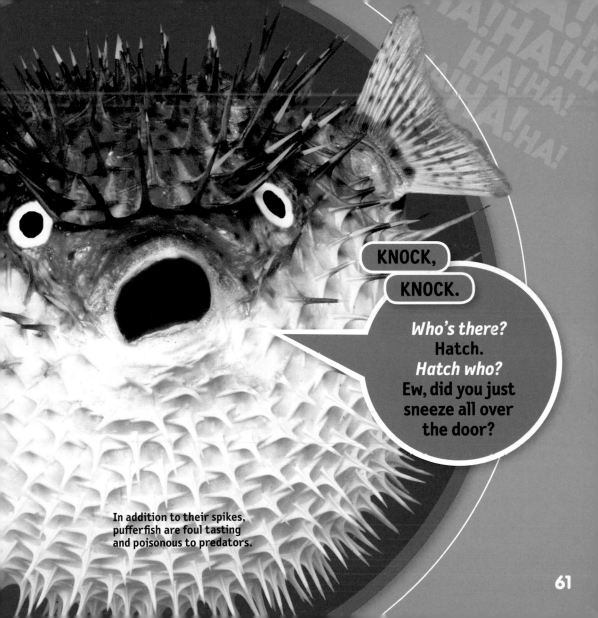

KNOCK, KNOCK.

Who's there?
Hatch.
Hatch who?
Ew, did you just sneeze all over the door?

In addition to their spikes, pufferfish are foul tasting and poisonous to predators.

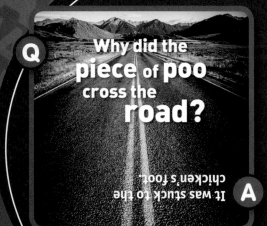

Q Why did the **piece** of **poo** **cross the** **road?**

A It was stuck to the chicken's foot.

Say this fast three times:

Michelle mashed **mosquitos,** making a **mosquito mush.**

Q How do you know if your armpits smell?

A Your teacher gives you extra points for not raising your hand in class.

Q What does an **oozing pimple** call her **pimple boyfriend?**

A Her main squeeze.

63

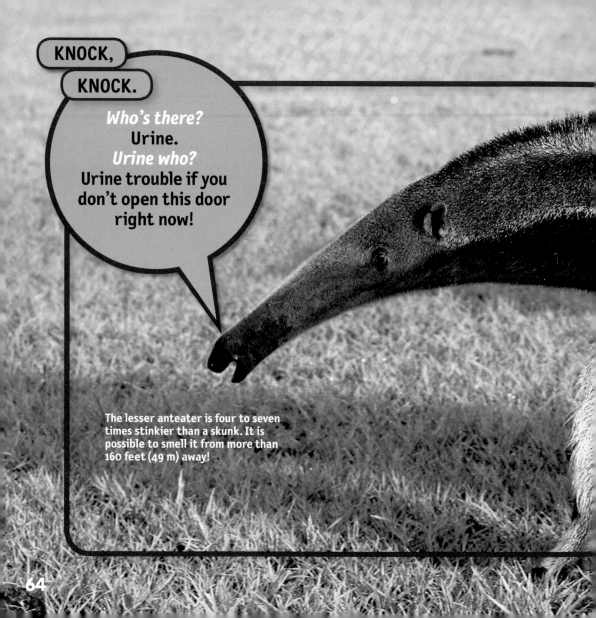

The lesser anteater is four to seven times stinkier than a skunk. It is possible to smell it from more than 160 feet (49 m) away!

Q Where do you buy rotten vegetables and stinky socks?

A The gross-ery store.

TRACEY: Did you hear about the giant that threw up?

FINNEGAN: No!

TRACEY: Really? It was all over town!

Q Why do you never want a clown to breathe on you?

A Because his breath smells funny.

TONGUE TWISTER!

Say this fast three times:

Fresh flounder fritters.

Q Why do skunks make great judges?

A Because they always have odor in the court.

Q What do you get if you cross a rear end and an ancient Roman fighter?

A A glut-iator.

71

OFFENSIVE OFFENDER:
Blobfish

FOUL FACTS:

The blobfish is exactly what its name sounds like! An animal made up of a jellylike substance, the blobfish has no bones, muscles, or teeth. This crazy creature may look like a pile of goo in photos, but normally, it's floating 2,000 to 3,900 feet (610–1,189 m) below sea level off the coast of Australia. In its natural habitat, scientists think the blobfish looks very different. The water pressure in the deep sea holds the animal's gelatinous body in shape, so the blobfish probably has a large head, tapered body, and a flat tail. It's only when this ocean animal is removed from that pressure that the blobfish slumps into a pile of ooze. Because blobfish live so far down in the depths, it's impossible to study them in their natural home.

World's Ugliest Animal

In 2013 the blobfish was voted the world's ugliest animal.

The blobfish is part of a family of animals called fatheads.

The blobfish can't actually swim. It just floats and sucks in whatever tasty meal passes by, such as tiny mollusks.

73

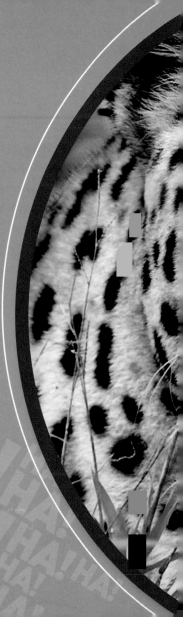

Q What do you get if you feed a group of kittens beans?

A A cat-toot-strophe.

MORTICIAN 1:
I think I'm going to quit my job.

MORTICIAN 2:
Why? I thought you enjoyed it?

MORTICIAN 1:
I do, but I have some stiff competition.

74

Cheetahs only drink water every three or four days.

KNOCK, KNOCK.

Who's there?
Saliva.
Saliva who?
Saliva feeling you aren't going to open the door.

75

Q

What do you get if you cross an officer and a dog?

A pooper trooper.

A

77

Q What do you get if you cross a mosquito and a lollipop?

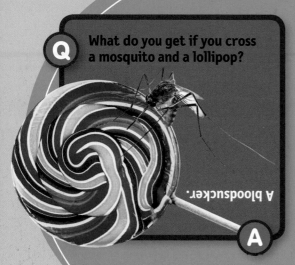

A A bloodsucker.

Say this fast three times:

Twisty tuna turd.

Q What is a man-eating monster's favorite meal?

A Feet-loaf and human beans with eyes-cream for dessert.

Q Why are false teeth like stars?

A Because they come out at night.

78

Millipedes protect themselves from predators by secreting a smelly liquid. One species oozes a poison that contains the powerful toxin cyanide.

KNOCK, KNOCK.
Who's there?
Aida.
Aida who?
Aida rotten egg and I think I'm going to hurl!

Q What **dinosaur** has the heathiest **teeth** and **gums?**

A The Floss-oraptor.

Q What do you call a **body builder** with the **flu?**

A Hurly burly.

80

Q

What is a
mosquito's
favorite
ice cream
flavor?

A Vein-illa.

Q What do you do if your nose goes on strike?

We are snot working!

Oh no, we won't blow!

A Picket.

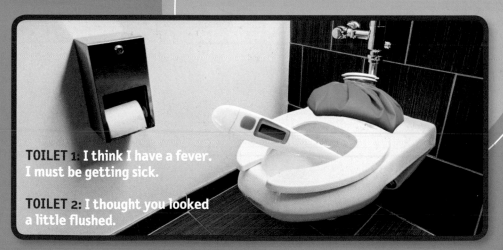

TOILET 1: I think I have a fever. I must be getting sick.

TOILET 2: I thought you looked a little flushed.

A great white shark's liver can be 24 percent of its total body weight.

KNOCK,
KNOCK.
Who's there?
Wire.
Wire who?
Wire you dancing?
Do you have
to pee?

Q

What do you give an elephant with an upset stomach?

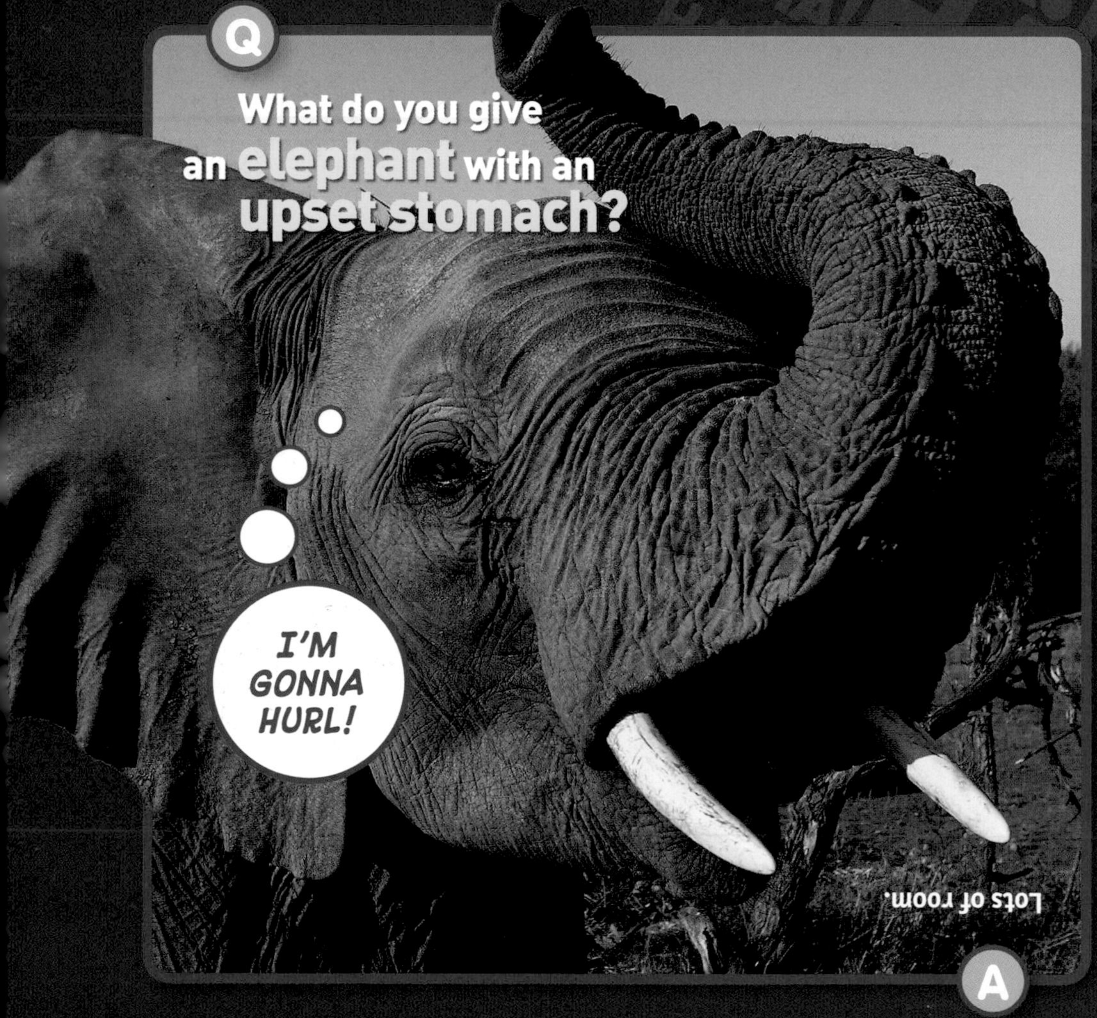

A

Lots of room.

Q What kind of luggage do hyenas take on vacation?

A Carrion.

Q What game do **zombies** play at **recess**?

A Corpse and Robbers.

87

Q Why did the centipede get kicked off the hockey team?

A It took too long to put its skates on.

Q What's the difference between boogers and Brussels sprouts?

A Kids don't eat Brussels sprouts.

Q What do you get if you eat an angry chicken?

A Fowl breath.

Q Why **can't** you **hear** a **pterodactyl** go to the **bathroom?**

A Because the *p* is silent.

Some species of goldfish don't have stomachs. This means that food moves swiftly through their digestive systems, and they create a lot of poop.

KNOCK, KNOCK.

Who's there?
Butter.
Butter who?
Butter open the door. It smells out here.

89

GIMME A KISS!

GROSS
ANIMALS

NAME Smiley

FAVORITE SAYING
Always make an
impression

FAVORITE HANGOUT
The dentist's office

PET PEEVE
Flossing

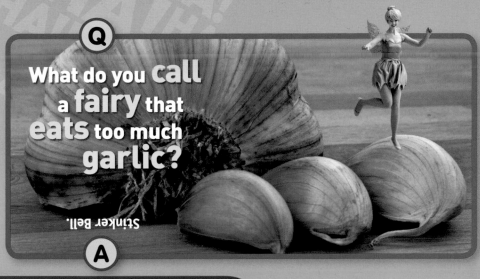

Q

What do you **call** a **fairy** that **eats** too much **garlic?**

Stinker Bell.

A

Funny names for boogers:

- Bats in the Bat Cave
- Snot Rockets
- The Schnozsquatch
- Nose Barnacle
- Nostril Cookies

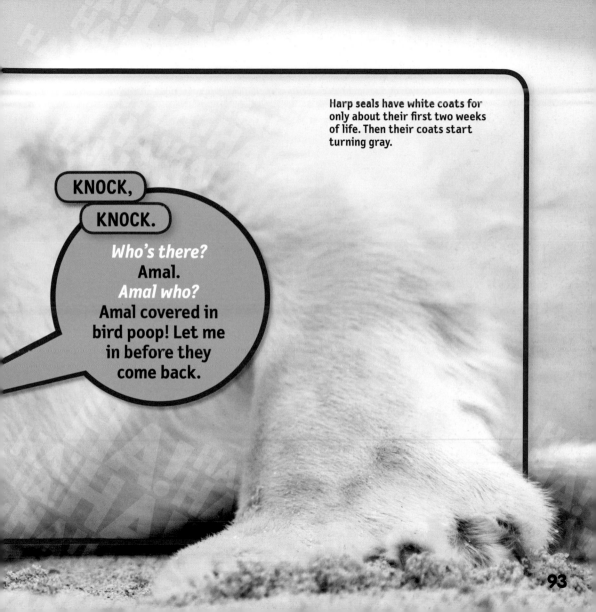

Harp seals have white coats for only about their first two weeks of life. Then their coats start turning gray.

KNOCK, KNOCK.

Who's there?
Amal.
Amal who?
Amal covered in bird poop! Let me in before they come back.

Grossest
of the Gross

OFFENSIVE OFFENDER:
The Gum Wall
FOUL FACTS:

Welcome to one of the grossest tourist attractions in the world! The Market Theater Gum Wall in Seattle, Washington, U.S.A., is a brick wall outside a theater that was covered in millions of pieces of used chewing gum. The gum was several inches thick in spots and covered an area about 50 feet (15 m) long by 15 feet (4.5 m) high. In 2015 the gum wall was cleaned off for the first time in 20 years. After about 130 hours of scraping and pressure washing, 2,350 pounds (1,066 kg) of gum was removed. So how do you dispose of a ton of ABC (Already Been Chewed) gum? Since gum isn't compostable and doesn't break down, it was packed into buckets and carted off to the local landfill. The wall didn't stay clean for long—less than a week later tourists and locals began re-gumming the sticky landmark, and the disgusting tradition continues.

In 2009 it was named the second germiest tourist attraction in the world.

Say cheese! The gum wall has been a popular destination for wedding photos.

The gum that was removed from the wall in 2015 filled 94 one-gallon buckets.

TONGUE TWISTER!

Say this fast three times:

Freshly fried fat frogs.

Q: What do you get if you cross a rose and a skunk?

A: I don't know but I wouldn't smell it.

Q: What kind of ice cream will make you sick?

A: Van-ill-a.

GROSS TALK

DUDE! YOU'RE GETTING SLOBBER ALL OVER MY BALL!

Q What do you get if you have 150 cockroaches in your kitchen?

A An infestation. Seriously, call an exterminator.

Q What happened when a giant pimple performed on stage?

A He received lots of ooze and ahs.

My dog's breath is so bad:

- When he barks, his teeth duck out of the way.

- He has to sneak up on his toothbrush.

- People look forward to his toots.

- His dentist quit.

- His tongue is planning its escape.

- People don't know if they should give him a breath mint or toilet paper.

TONGUE TWISTER!

Say this fast three times:

Prickly, pointy poop projecting posteriorly.

Q

Which animal will always barf on an amusement park ride?

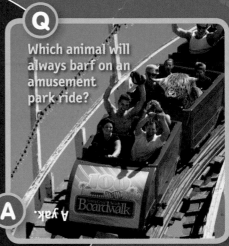

A A yak.

Q

Why did the executioner go to work early?

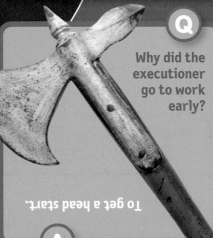

To get a head start.

A

Q

What is a slug's favorite meal?

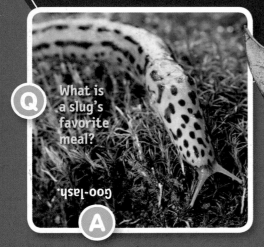

Goo-lash.

A

Grizzly bears give birth in their sleep while hibernating.

KNOCK, KNOCK.

Who's there?
Thumpin'.
Thumpin' who?
Thumpin' green is hanging out of your nose.

103

GROSS TALK

105

Q What do you get if you cross a cockroach and a horse?

A A bugging bronco.

FRANK: Do you always eat cockroaches?

JOANNE: No! Why do you ask?

FRANK: Because one just crawled into your sandwich.

KNOCK, KNOCK.

Who's there?
Wilfred.
Wilfred who?
Wilfred please take off his shoes? I think he stepped in something ...

Ostriches swallow stones to help them digest their food.

107

Why did the
toilet paper
roll down
a **hill?**

What do you get if you cross a
pig and a portable bathroom?

Because it wanted to
get to the bottom.

A

A pork-a-potty.

A

NAME Kit E. Litter

FAVORITE SAYING
Try to think outside
the box

FAVORITE PASTIME
Watching humans
clean my litter box

PET PEEVE
Hair balls

GROSS
ANIMALS

109

Q

What's **brown** and **spins** around a child's **waist?**

A A hula poop.

Say this fast three times:

Violent Violet vomits vicious vapors.

Q

What do you get if you cross a turkey and a centipede?

Drumsticks for everyone!

A

Q

What do you get if you cross a skunk and a pachyderm?

A smelly-phant.

A

110

Alligators can digest anything they swallow, but sometimes they need more than 13 days to digest bones.

Q

What do you get if you cross a sneeze and a tiny dog?

A

Achoo-wawa.

GHOST 1: Where are you going?
GHOST 2: My friend is taking me for a jog.
GHOST 1: It's about time you were exorcised.

114

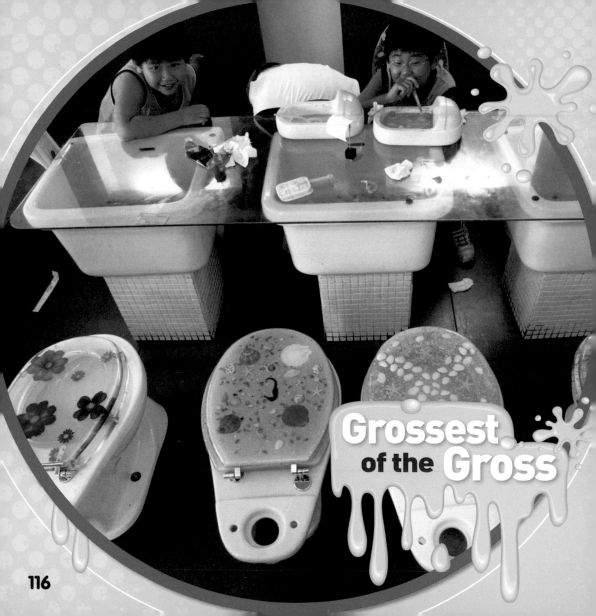

Grossest
of the Gross

OFFENSIVE OFFENDER:
Toilet Restaurant
FOUL FACTS:

In Kaohsiung City, Taiwan, you can visit a three-story toilet-themed restaurant. The restaurant is decorated like a bathroom, with plunger- and poo-shaped lights on the ceiling, tables made of glass-covered sinks or bathtubs, showerhead artwork on the walls, and a giant golden turd that greets you at the door. Diners sit on actual toilets (don't worry, they don't work), and their meals are served in miniature toilet bowls. Thirsty? Why not order a drink in a tiny plastic urinal that you can take home as a souvenir? The owner of the restaurant came up with the idea after the success of his ice-cream shop, where he sold swirls of chocolate ice cream served in mini toilets. He now owns 12 toilet-themed restaurants in Taiwan and Hong Kong.

If you need a napkin you will find a roll of toilet paper hanging over your table.

The restaurant is named Matong, after the Chinese word for toilet.

Got a sweet tooth? Why not try the "green dysentery" ice cream served in a squat-style toilet bowl?

Q What Spanish city is full of people with the flu?

A Barf-elona.

Say this fast three times:

Blueberry booger bubbles.

Q What happened when the singer passed gas on stage?

A She blew everyone away.

Q What do you get if you cross a bear and a skunk?

A Winnie the Pee-yew.

118

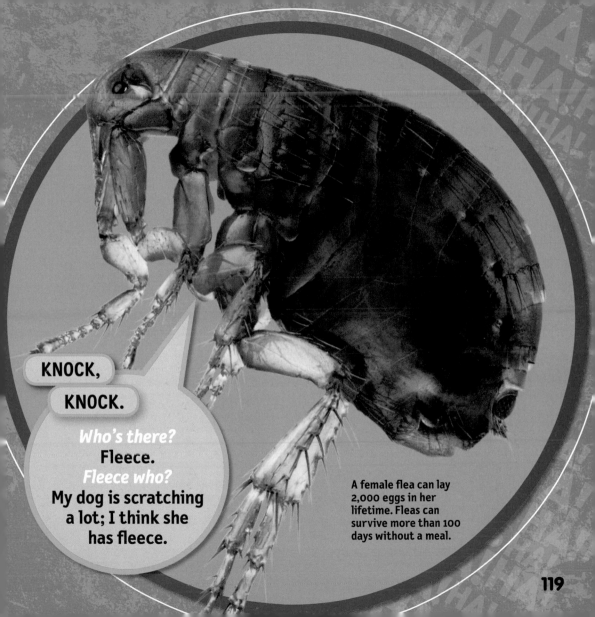

KNOCK, KNOCK.

Who's there?
Fleece.
Fleece who?
My dog is scratching a lot; I think she has fleece.

A female flea can lay 2,000 eggs in her lifetime. Fleas can survive more than 100 days without a meal.

HA! HA! HA! HA! HA!
I'M SORRY! I DIDN'T KNOW I WAS GOING TO TOOT! COME BACK!
Gross TALK

Q What did the owner say to her puppy after it peed on the floor?

A "Urine trouble!"

Q What did one bag of garbage say to the other bag of garbage?

A "Go get dressed up. They are taking us out."

Q What do you get if you cross an earthworm and a hippopotamus?

A Very big holes in your garden.

Q How do fleas travel from one place to another?

A By itch-hiking.

Some toads secrete a poison that can cause convulsions, paralysis, or death in predators.

123

NAME **Trash Can**

FAVORITE CHORE
Cleaning up after big dinners

FAVORITE HANGOUT
The buffet

PET PEEVE
Sharing

Q

What do you call a skinny booger?

A

Slim pickins.

GRAVEDIGGER 1: Who's coming to your party?
GRAVEDIGGER 2: Oh, anyone I can dig up.

Lions mark their territory with pungent urine. They also pee backward!

127

My cat is so dirty:

- She has to creep up on bathwater.
- A skunk smelled her and passed out.
- She fertilizes the lawn by rolling in it.
- When she plays in a sandbox, other cats bury her.
- Her washcloth begged for mercy.

Q What's **yellow, sticky,** and smells like **bananas?**

A Monkey snot.

Q Why did the girl bring **toilet paper** to a **birthday celebration?**

A Because she was a party pooper.

130

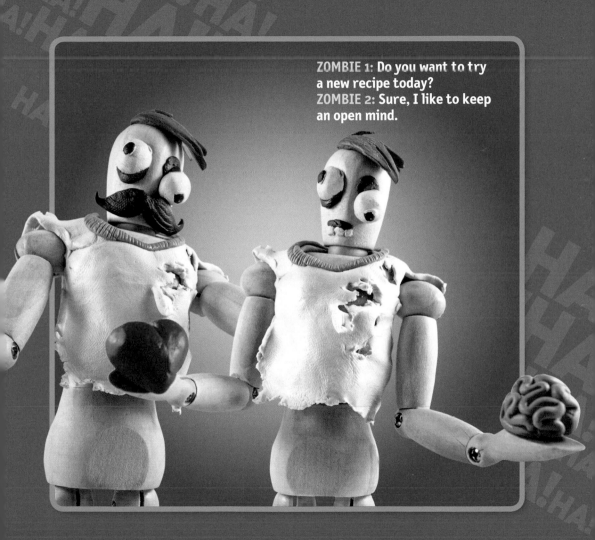

Q What's **brown** and **sticky?**

A A stick.

Say this fast three times:

This **pooper scooper** sure scoops **super.**

Q What do you get if you cross a rear end and a servant?

A A butt-ler.

Q What has **four legs,** a long **tail,** and **flies?**

A A dead rat.

Viper venom can sometimes cause necrosis, or the death of cells in tissue and muscles, in bite victims.

133

What do you call ghost vomit?

Q

Spook puke.

A

Wolverines can emit a nasty-smelling spray to scare off predators. They also spray it on their leftovers so nothing else comes along and eats them.

I STOPPED TO TIE UP MY SHOELACES AND MISSED MY BUS!

137

Grossest
of the Gross

OFFENSIVE OFFENDER:
The Hairy Frog (or Horror Frog)

FOUL FACTS:

What has razor-sharp claws, hair made of skin, and hops? It sounds like the makings of a supervillain, but it is actually *Trichobatrachus robustus*, otherwise known as the hairy frog. The male of the species grows long, hairlike strands of skin and arteries on its sides and thighs. After females lay eggs, the males stay with the eggs. It's thought that the "hairs" help absorb more oxygen while the frogs are taking care of their young. If that's not gruesome enough, the hairy frog can break its own bones and force the sharpened fragments through the skin of its back feet to create claws. The horror frog certainly lives up to its name!

The hairy frog is roasted and eaten in Cameroon.

Hairy frog tadpoles are very aggressive and have multiple rows of horned teeth.

The hairy frog is also referred to as Wolverine frog—which is a reference to the comic book superhero Wolverine, from *X-Men*, who sports retractable claws.

DUNG BEETLE 1: It was nice visiting with you. Are you sure you have to leave now?
DUNG BEETLE 2: Yeah, I gotta roll.

Q

What do you get when a dinosaur blows his nose?

A

Out of the way.

Q

What game do **vampires** like to **play?**

A

Follow the bleeder.

Q

What do you get if you cross a tarantula and a bushel of apples?

A

Apple spider.

What is a
butterfly's
best subject in
school?

Moth-ematics.

A

143

Q What's worse than finding a worm in your apple?

A Finding half a worm.

HOW AM I GOING TO WORM MY WAY OUT OF THIS ONE?

Gross TALK

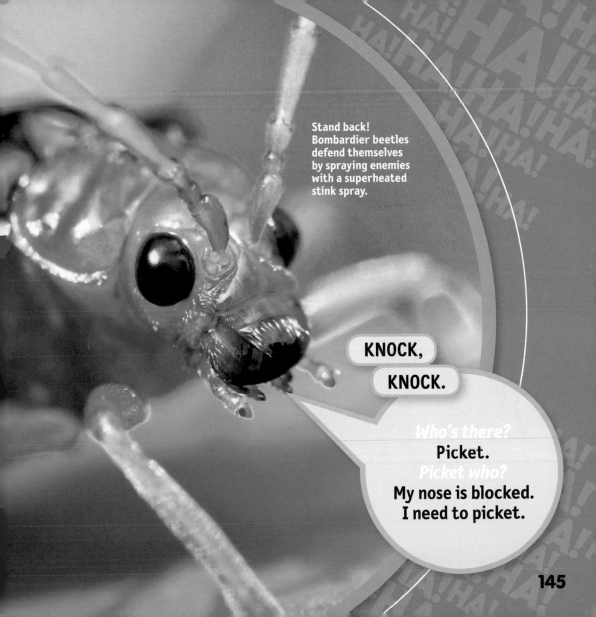

Stand back! Bombardier beetles defend themselves by spraying enemies with a superheated stink spray.

KNOCK, KNOCK.

Who's there?
Picket.
Picket who?
My nose is blocked.
I need to picket.

145

GROSS TALK

DUDE, FOR THE LAST TIME, I'M NOT SMELLING YOUR BREATH!

146

Q What do you call head lice on a bald man?

A Homeless.

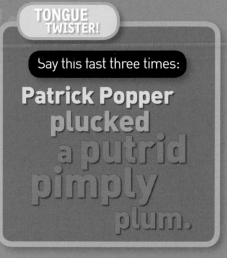

Say this fast three times:

Patrick Popper plucked a putrid pimply plum.

Q What do you call a ghost that picks its nose?

A The boogie monster.

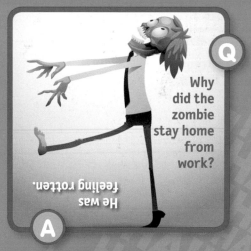

Q Why did the zombie stay home from work?

A He was feeling rotten.

147

Q What do you get if you cross a cow and a head cold?

A Lots of moo-cus.

TONGUE TWISTER!

Say this fast three times:

Shirley's shop sells short, smelly socks.

Q What do you get if you cross a parrot and a buffalo?

A I don't know but I don't want to clean the cage.

Q Why did the **zombies** go to a **party?**

A Because they like to meat people.

150

A skunk's spray can cause temporary blindness.

KNOCK, KNOCK.

Who's there? Giant stinky skunk ... Hello? ... Hello?

151

Whale sharks are followed by remoras, which clean the sharks' skin and eat parasites that live on their bodies.

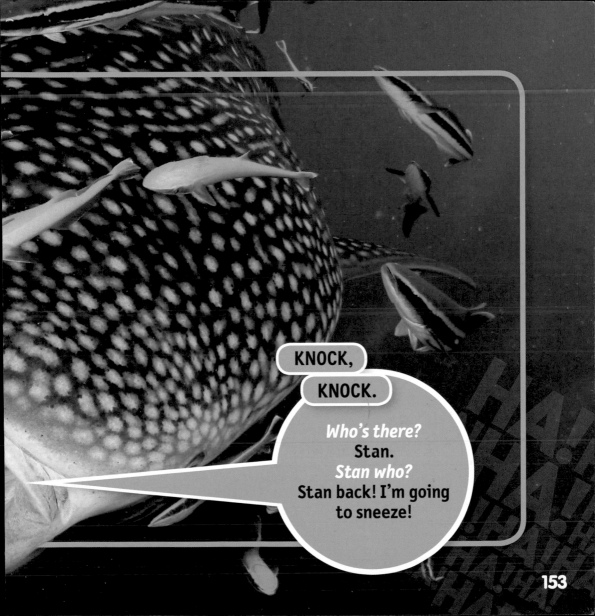

153

DINER: Waiter, there's a cockroach in my soup!

WAITER: Sorry, sir, we ran out of flies.

Q

What do you call a dinosaur with the flu?

A

Tyrannosaurus retch.

155

Q What do you call a pig with a runny nose?

A A ham-booger.

MMMM, SALTY!

Gross TALK

156

KNOCK, KNOCK.

Who's there?
Consumption.
Consumption who?
Consumption be done about all the garbage around here? It stinks.

In some countries, scorpions are sold as street food and are served on a stick.

AHHH ... NOTHING FEELS BETTER THAN SCRATCHING THAT HARD-TO-REACH ITCH.

OFFENSIVE OFFENDER:
Filthy Flies
FOUL FACTS:

Despite being disease-spreading, germ-carrying pests, flies are one of the most important insects in the world. They have a very crucial role to play in our ecosystem by breaking down and eating decaying organic matter, feces, and animal remains. This creates new top soil, which allows new plants to grow. Flies even help pollinate flowers and plants. Sure, a single fly can carry around a million germs on its body and spread illnesses like typhoid to humans, but without them, the world would have one big trash problem on its hands.

During the American Civil War, blowfly maggots, or fly larvae, were placed in soldiers' wounds to eat the dead tissue and pus to clear up infections.

A fly will secrete saliva and vomit onto its food to help liquefy it and then suck it up with its proboscis. Keep that in mind the next time one lands on your lunch!

A fly poops every four to five minutes.

Q Where should you bring a bee with the flu?

A To the wasp-ital.

Q What's the difference between a **centipede** and a **cockroach?**

A Cockroaches crunch more when you eat them.

162

163

Q

What do you get if you put a cat's litter box in the freezer?

A

Poop-cicles.

Q

What kind of
citrus fruit does
a vampire eat?

A

Blood
oranges
and
neck-tarines.

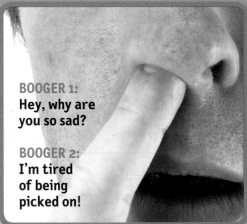

BOOGER 1:
Hey, why are
you so sad?

BOOGER 2:
I'm tired
of being
picked on!

KNOCK, KNOCK.

Who's there?
Goo.
Goo who?
I came for a visit.
I had no other place
to goo.

Chinese water dragons have a "third eye" on the top of their heads that helps them regulate their body temperature.

167

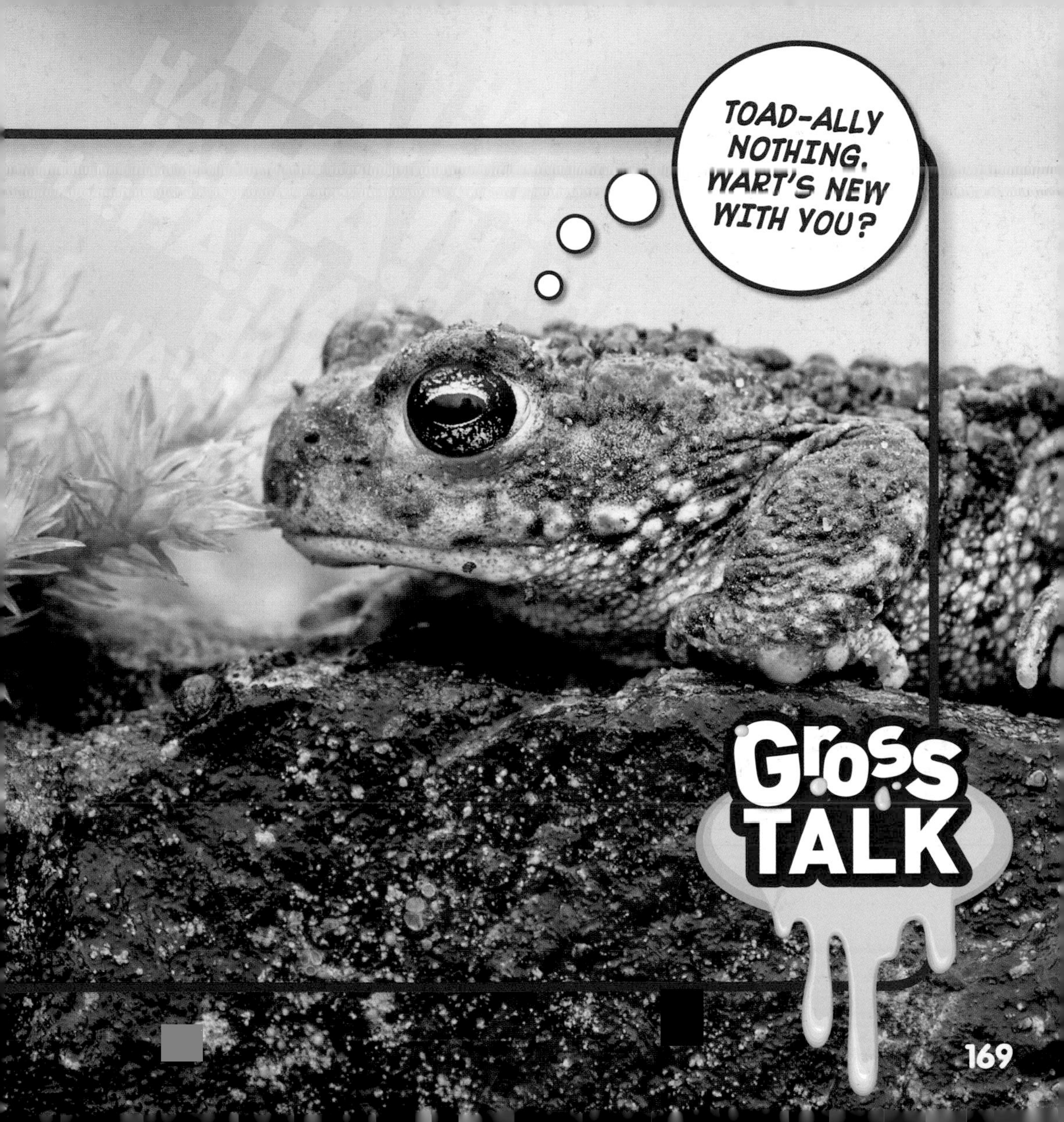
TOAD-ALLY NOTHING. WART'S NEW WITH YOU?
GROSS TALK

My bedroom is so messy:

- You have to wipe your feet before you go outside.
- The roaches sent me an eviction notice.
- The ants bring napkins so they don't have to eat off the floor.

PIG 1: Where are you going to buy your Christmas gifts?
PIG 2: At the slopping mall.

What does the dentist of the year receive?

Q

A little plaque.

A

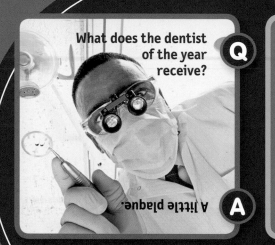

TONGUE TWISTER!

Say this fast three times:

Countless clams crammed in a clean creamed-clam can.

Do zombies like the dark?

Q

Of corpse they do!

A

What's the difference between a dinner plate and a booger?

Q

The plate is on the table, but the booger is under the table.

A

172

Otters use rocks to smash open clams and mussels.

KNOCK, KNOCK.

Who's there?
Indigestion.
Indigestion who?
To be or not to be, that's indigestion.

173

Gross TALK

WHY DO I ALWAYS ORDER THE NUMBER 2 MEAL?

Gross TALK

Q Where did the ghost go on vacation?

A The Dead Sea.

TONGUE TWISTER!

Say this fast three times:

Derek drains dirty ditches.

Q How did the skunk phone his mother?

A On his smell phone.

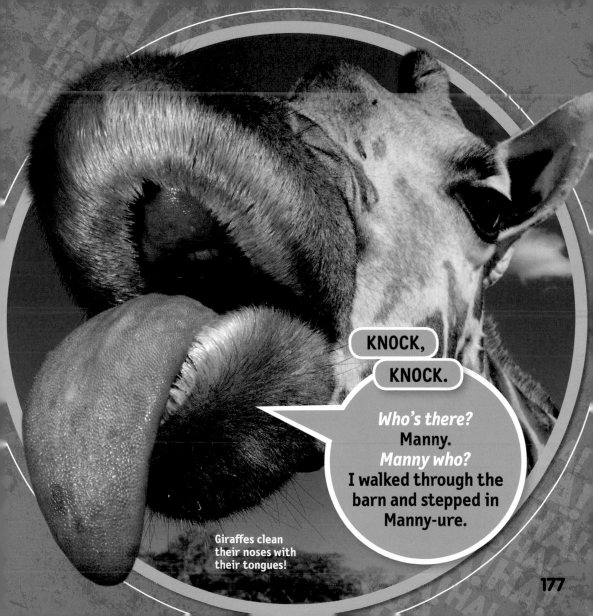

Giraffes clean their noses with their tongues!

177

Q

What did the
spider bride
wear to the
ceremony?

A webbing dress.

A

Q What do you get if you cross a nut and a toilet?

A A pee-can.

Q Why did the **driver** toot in her **wallet?**

A She needed gas money.

Alpacas will sometimes spit half-digested green gobs of goo as a sign of dominance.

181

Grossest
of the Gross

OFFENSIVE OFFENDER:
Eyelash Mites

FOUL FACTS:

Say hello to my little friend ... or hundreds of little friends. *Demodex folliculorum* are tiny mites that live on your face, specifically on your eyelashes. They spend their time buried head-down in your eyelash follicles, feeding on the dead skin and fluids that build up there. Eyelash mites prefer to live on areas of human skin covered in oil, called sebum, which is why they love living in the hair follicles on your face. Their numbers are also higher in the summer when hot temperatures increase sebum production.

There can be more than 25 mites on a single eyelash follicle.

Eyelash mites never poop—instead they release a lifetime's worth of waste when they die.

Mites are relatives of ticks, spiders, and scorpions.

Q What kind of **clothing** do you wear to a **manure factory?**

A Dung-arees.

Say this fast three times:

Pete's peppy **puppy** produced **piles** of **poop.**

Q What color is a belch?

A Burple.

Q What do you call a blood-sucking bug in France?

A Paris-ite.

Centipedes will often sacrifice some of their limbs to escape being eaten, leaving birds with a beak full of legs instead of a tasty meal. Centipedes can then regrow any legs they lost in the getaway.

KNOCK, KNOCK.

Who's there?
Ice cream.
Ice cream who?
Ice cream if you don't get this centipede off me!

Why are frogs so happy?

Because they eat
whatever bugs them.

A

187

Q What do you get if you cross Rice Krispies and a diaper?

A Snap, crackle, poop.

Q What do you get if you cross a cut on your knee and a magic trick?

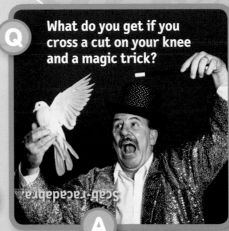

A Scab-racadabra.

Q What's invisible and smells like peanuts?

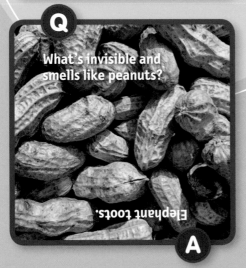

A Elephant toots.

Q What is a snail's favorite drink?

A Slime-aid.

Some tarantula species can "shoot" barbed hairs from their abdomens to defend themselves. These hairs can create a burning sensation to the unlucky victim.

KNOCK, KNOCK.

Who's there?
Sara.
Sara who?
Sara exterminator in the house? There are spiders everywhere!

190

Q What kind of **jam** can't be eaten?

A Toe jam.

Q What kind of **flowers** do you bring to a **frog's** funeral?

A A croak-us.

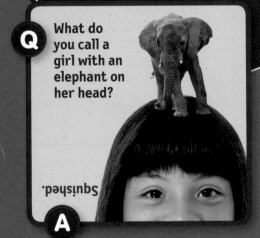

Q What do you call a girl with an elephant on her head?

A Squished.

Q Why do **leeches** make great **employees?**

A Because they get attached to their work.

Hairless cats require more baths than their furry cousins. A residue of oil, sweat, and saliva builds up on their skin because there is no hair to absorb it.

KNOCK, KNOCK.

Who's there?
Falafel.
Falafel who?
I drank some spoiled milk and now I falafel.

193

Grossest of the Gross

OFFENSIVE OFFENDER:

Icky Earwax

FOUL FACTS:

If you've got ears, you've got earwax, and you should be happy you do. Earwax is not really wax—it's made up of sloughed skin cells, dirt, and dust, and its official name is cerumen. It may be disgusting, but it has an important job to do. Earwax traps and prevents bacteria and other microorganisms from entering your ear and causing infections. It also moisturizes the ear canal so your ears don't feel dry or itchy. Ears are even self-cleaning! Earwax will slowly work itself out of the ear canal while you are chewing or talking, then dry up and flake off or fall out.

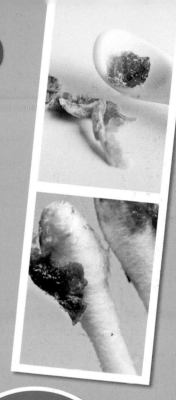

In the 1800s, earwax was commonly used as lip balm.

Before waxed thread was invented, seam-stresses used earwax to stop the ends of threads from fraying.

In 2007 a 10-inch (25-cm)-long plug of earwax was removed from the ear canal of a dead blue whale that washed up on a California, U.S.A., beach. That's almost as wide as a football!

Deep-sea anglerfish have huge stomachs and massive mouths. They can swallow prey up to twice their own size.

197

Funny names for bad breath:

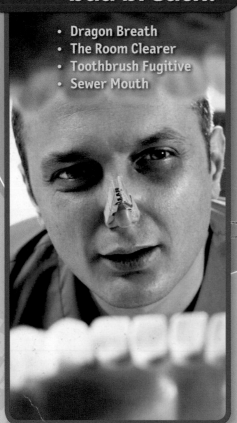

- Dragon Breath
- The Room Clearer
- Toothbrush Fugitive
- Sewer Mouth

TERMITE: I love hanging out with you.
COCKROACH: You are my pest friend!

KNOCK, KNOCK.

Who's there?
Police.
Police who?
Police brush your teeth—your breath is awful!

A vulture will urinate on its own legs to cool itself down if it's too hot. This also helps kill any bacteria it may be carrying around from stepping in rotten carcasses while eating.

A hippo's sweat not only prevents sunburns, it also protects the hippo from absorbing any toxins from the water it swims in.

JOKEFINDER

JOKEFINDER

Tongue twisters

ILLUSTRATIONCREDITS

Since 1888, the National Geographic Society has funded more than 12,000
research, exploration, and preservation projects around the world. The
Society receives funds from National Geographic Partners, LLC, funded in
part by your purchase. A portion of the proceeds from this book supports
this vital work. To learn more, visit natgeo.com/info.

NATIONAL GEOGRAPHIC and Yellow Border Design are trademarks of the
National Geographic Society, used under license.

For more information, visit nationalgeographic.com, call 1-800-647-5463,
or write to the following address:
National Geographic Partners
1145 17th Street N.W.
Washington, D.C. 20036-4688 U.S.A.

Visit us online at nationalgeographic.com/books

For librarians and teachers: ngchildrensbooks.org

More for kids from National Geographic: kids.nationalgeographic.com

For information about special discounts for bulk purchases, please contact
National Geographic Books Special Sales: specialsales@natgeo.com

For rights or permissions inquiries, please contact National Geographic
Books Subsidiary Rights: bookrights@natgeo.com

Art directed by Callie Broaddus
Editorial, Design, and Production by Plan B Book Packagers

Trade paperback ISBN: 978-1-4263-2717-9
Reinforced library edition ISBN: 978-1-4263-2718-6

Printed in China
16/PPS/1